HOPSCOTCH
TWISTY TALES

Puss in Football Boots

by Sam Watkins and O'Kif

W
FRANKLIN WATTS
LONDON•SYDNEY

This story is based on the traditional fairy tale,
Puss in Boots, but with a new twist.
You can read the original story in
Must Know Stories. Can you make
up your own twist for the story?

Franklin Watts
First published in Great Britain in 2016 by The Watts Publishing Group

Text © Sam Watkins 2016
Illustrations © O'Kif 2016

The rights of Sam Watkins to be identified as the author
and O'Kif as the illustrator of this Work have been asserted
in accordance with the Copyright, Designs and Patents Act, 1988.

ISBN 978 1 4451 4794 9 (hbk)
ISBN 978 1 4451 4796 3 (pbk)
ISBN 978 1 4451 4795 6 (library ebook)

Series Editor: Melanie Palmer
Series Advisor: Catherine Glavina
Series Designer: Peter Scoulding
Cover Designer: Cathryn Gilbert

Printed in China

Franklin Watts
An imprint of
Hachette Children's Group
Part of The Watts Publishing Group
Carmelite House
50 Victoria Embankment
London EC4Y 0DZ

An Hachette UK Company
www.hachette.co.uk

www.franklinwatts.co.uk

MIX
Paper from
responsible sources
FSC® C104740
FSC
www.fsc.org

Once upon a half-time, there was
a football-mad lad called Jack.

He longed to play for Fabchester United. For his birthday, he asked his gran for a new football kit.

When the day came, he opened Gran's present.

"Miaoowwww!"

A ginger cat jumped out!

"Gran! I said *kit* not *kitten*," said Jack. "What use is a flea-ridden old cat?"

"Old? The cheek!" miaowed the cat. "I'm a lot of use, actually. I'll help you play for Fabchester United. But you must give me something in return."

Jack looked at the cat, surprised.

"What do you want?"

"A pair of football boots," replied the cat.

"Okay," Jack said. He found an old pair of boots and gave them to the cat.

They fitted purr-fectly!

"I'll call you Puss-in-Football-Boots," said Jack. "Puss for short."

Puss went to Jack's next match.
Jack fell over five times and scored
an own goal.

As the final whistle blew, Jack slumped to the ground.

"A talent scout from Fabchester United is coming next week," he told Puss. "He's going to pick one player. But if I play like I did today I haven't got a chance!"

"Don't panic," Puss purred. "At the next game, do everything I tell you. And whatever you do, DON'T go in the changing rooms."

CHANGING ROOM 1

19

The following Saturday, Jack wore his kit to the match. When he went onto the pitch he saw the talent scout watching.

Jack gulped. This was his chance…

21

PHEEEEEEEP! The ref blew
the whistle.

To Jack's astonishment, all the other players started hopping around scratching themselves! "GO, JACK!" miaowed Puss.

Jack pounced on the ball and ran up the pitch.

He dodged players from the other team, who were rolling around on the ground, scratching frantically.

The goal was in his sights...

"SHOOT!" he heard Puss miaow.

He aimed ... he shot ... he scored!

"MIAOWWWW!" miaowed Puss.
"WHOOP, WHOOP!" cheered the
crowd. SCRATCH, SCRATCH,
SCRATCH went the
other players.

The talent scout was impressed. Next week Jack got to play for Fabchester United. He was soon playing big matches alongside all his favourite (if sometimes a bit itchy) players.

And Jack never called Puss old
or flea-ridden again!

Puzzle 1

Put these pictures in the correct order.
Which event do you think is most important?
Now try writing the story in your own words!

Puzzle 2

1. I am good at solving problems.

2. I need lots of football practice.

3. I need a new kit.

4. I am very cunning and crafty!

5. I want to play better.

6. I like helping people.

Choose the correct speech bubbles for each character. Can you think of any others? Turn over to find the answers.

Answers

Puzzle 1

The correct order is: 1b, 2f, 3d, 4e, 5a, 6c

Puzzle 2

Jack: 2, 3, 5

Puss: 1, 4, 6

Look out for more Hopscotch Twisty Tales

The Ninjabread Man
ISBN 978 1 4451 3964 7
The Boy Who Cried Sheep!
ISBN 978 1 4451 4292 0
Thumbelina Thinks Big
ISBN 978 1 4451 4295 1
**Move versus the
Enormous Turnip**
ISBN 978 1 4451 4300 2
Big Pancacke to the Rescue
ISBN 978 1 4451 4303 3
Little Red Hen's Great Escape
ISBN 978 1 4451 4305 7
The Lovely Duckling
ISBN 978 1 4451 1633 4
**Hansel and Gretel
and the Green Witch**
ISBN 978 1 4451 1634 1
The Emperor's New Kit
ISBN 978 1 4451 1635 8

**Rapunzel and the
Prince of Pop**
ISBN 978 1 4451 1636 5
**Dick Whittington
Gets on his Bike**
ISBN 978 1 4451 1637 2
**The Pied Piper and
the Wrong Song**
ISBN 978 1 4451 1638 9
**The Princess and the
Frozen Peas**
ISBN 978 1 4451 0675 5
Snow White Sees the Light
ISBN 978 1 4451 0676 2
**The Elves and the
Trendy Shoes**
ISBN 978 1 4451 0678 6
The Three Frilly Goats Fluff
ISBN 978 1 4451 0677 9

Princess Frog
ISBN 978 1 4451 0679 3
Rumpled Stilton Skin
ISBN 978 1 4451 0680 9
Jack and the Bean Pie
ISBN 978 1 4451 0182 8
**Brownilocks and the Three
Bowls of Cornflakes**
ISBN 978 1 4451 0183 5
Cinderella's Big Foot
ISBN 978 1 4451 0184 2
Little Bad Riding Hood
ISBN 978 1 4451 0185 9
**Sleeping Beauty –
100 Years Later**
ISBN 978 1 4451 0186 6
**The Three Little Pigs &
the New Neighbour**
ISBN 978 1 4451 0181 1